# The Blossoms of the
# Night-Blooming Cereus

A poetry collection by

Ursula T. Gibson

PublishAmerica
Baltimore

First printing

Cover photography by James Gibson.

ISBN: 1-4137-6482-7
PUBLISHED BY PUBLISHAMERICA, LLLP
www.publishamerica.com
Baltimore

Printed in the United States of America

## Dedication and Acknowledgments

Without James Gibson's existence, many of these poems would never have been written. His quiet encouragement and participation in the love of this art form has been vital. Not only has he provided the living experiences, the scenery, the adventures, and the pride in our work, but he has created thirty-seven years of love and a forwarding-looking life for us. That provides a safe haven from which to explore the turbulance and the magnificence of living and makes possible a review of both the the difficult and the pleasant aspects of life, which is a poet's job.

I thank my editors and publisher for creation of this book. Their skill and effort have turned mere words on a page into an item of beauty.

I thank my teachers, Dorothy Willard, deceased, Los Angeles High School, 1945–1948; Dorothy Kaucher, Ph.D., deceased, and Edward Miller, Ph.D., San Jose State College 1949–1952 (now San Jose State University), San Jose, California, who taught me what poetry is about and valued my attempts; my son, Rudolf Shouldice, deceased, who opened my eyes to the future; and my friends and members of California Federation of Chaparral Poets, Inc., who for years have listened to my writing struggles and revisions with understanding and patience.

Ursula T. Gibson

# Table of Contents

# Why I Write Poetry

There's this Muse, see?
She curiously pokes in on me
at odd hours of day or night
to peer at words. I'm not too bright
at figuring out her meaning
in all this word-search gleaning,
so she kicks and whines
achieving almost a tantrum rage,
'til my attention and her tension
are aligned, words rush to the page,
without grace or dignity, not to mention
skill, poetic device, or proper lines.

When that Muse is satisfied then,
treated to an adult's literary agony,
keeping up with her intensity—when
exhaustion overcomes my creativity,
and she goes off to plague some other
victim, I read again what she provoked,
tamp out the twentieth cigarette I've smoked,
tweak and tune, sort, revise and bother
to hammer out, word by word, line by line
the poems you get to see as mine.

Ursula T. Gibson, 1-13-01, rev. 8-8-04.

## Colors of the Rainbow

You are! and rainbow colors fill my mind.
The ecstasy and wonder
that you and I should bind
our thoughts, never to be asunder,
leap in dazzling blaze of light
from your strong fervor
to color my pastel nights
and make me believe "forever"!

Ursula T. Gibson, 5-6-88

## Crushed Sand

Savage sounds slashing the air,
Chaos of cause and effect,
Intimidating eyes glaring,
Harassing hands gesturing,
Overriding all dignity,
Stripping me of logic and love,
Incomprehensible anger,
Like a manic-depressive crisis;
Like storm waves lashing a shoreline.

But, like rolling sand under the wave,
I resist the onslaught,
Letting it slide unchanging over me,
Just moving a little, turning a little,
'Til the storm passes, and all is still.

The weather around you is changeable,
Unpredictable, frightful with thunder.
As sand, I could survive a while,
But each roll exposes another
Facet of me to your grinding,
Relentless ripping away of value
Until all that I am is destroyed.

What use is a characterless
Grain of sand? What use will I be to you
When I have been ground to powder?
Why do you need to thunder?

# EYES

I am most in love with you
When our eyes meet, and you smile
As though the contact of our souls
Was pleasurable and necessary.

To watch your being awake to me
And know you care, sends waves
Of yearning through me; I respond
To that deep light of love in your eyes,

More than your hand's warm touch
Or your kiss, blender though that be,
Enmeshing me in your existence.
It is your soul in your eyes I love.

## WATTS—1965

My little son and I lived among a block of folks
in South Central Los Angeles.
Seven years of coming and going,
recipes and stories exchanged over the fence,
and walks around the block,
waving to white-haired elderly
sitting on their evening verandas,
with a word or two on Sundays
about the goodness of the Lord.

My son played up and down the block,
with countless little ones like him,
spacemen and monsters,
cowboys and Indians (he was the Indian)
rode his bike in tandem with his friends.
All of them parked outside our door
for milk and cookies, and the bikes
were safely left, day or night.

On Sundays in the nearby tiny park,
a corner bit of green with trees and benches,
I sat with other mothers,
watching our busy children play.
We traded information on
how to get them to eat vegetables,
to pick up their toys, to listen,
where to buy good clothes for cheap,
why the rents were going up.
I wrote letters for those who wanted
to reach back home but could not write.
We shared our money for hot dogs
and ice cream all around,
like neighbors do. Just like neighbors do.                >>

13

Oh, it wasn't all idyllic;
there were interruptions of calm
by anger and shouting when a lover
got jealous or a woman ran from knifethrust
of her drunken man to my strong screen door
and safety inside, weeping,
to tell me misunderstanding:
"He was a good man, but under the weather,
you know?" while I, hugging her
and wiping tears away, bit my lips
at life's cruelty and fear,
made coffee, tea or cocoa for both of us
to sip away our terror at love mislaid.
We shared those sorrows, seeking ways to heal.

When I was spent or frightened,
I'd turn to Jennie or Mildred,
Marnesba or Sally Ann, and they'd listen
wisely and point out my folly or my future,
always true and fair.
We were all friends on my block, all friends.

The fire alarms and shrieking sirens,
black smoke from burning buildings,
were the first I knew of Watts:
five days of black fury and frustration,
hurling fire at injustice, voicing hatred,
practicing destruction.
From August 11 to August 16 on our block,
all doors were closed, faces peering warily
past lifted curtains at hasty sirens
screaming past, fired-up shouts of anger.
Cars hurried past; no one dared to walk
the streets those five long days,
except the shouting, angry men in a cloud

like fire smoke up and down the streets,
breaking windows, destroying cars and stores,
dragging fear and separation with them.

When it was over, next day,
I went outside again and walked around
our block. No one spoke to me.
No one waved. No one.

Only then, when Watts happened,
only then, I learned I was white.

Ursula T. Gibson, © December 1989; rev. 8-10-04

**Fashion**

It's been my cynical opinion that
to get the jump on next year's fashion moguls,
go and visit your local
red light district and study
what the prostitutes are wearing,
how they look and make themselves up.
*There* are next year's fashions.

Ursula T. Gibson, 6-3-99

## Repulsive

(written when I weighed 341 pounds)

I hate the fat, the tangible
grease at the creases of my thighs
when I have sweated, and the oily
sheen of my face in the morning
before I rush to soap to bring control.
Sitting down, the forty pounds of
my abdomen spread over my thigh-tops;
I see the stretched maw of my navel
like a yawn.

I hate taking baths in which
a quarter of the tub is water
and the rest is me,
or showers in which I brace
against the wall to clean my heels and toes,
one foot at a time, bent forward,
shoving fat aside to get a better grip.

I hate the fat in elevator mirror images or
sleek polished stone building faces, in which
I am lost in one hundred forty extra pounds
I lug along, front and back, top to bottom,
an edifice of triglycerides.

I hate marks of creases where fat joins muscle
and sags beyond the limits,
my breasts that drag downward despite bras
to meet my bulging stomach.                >>

I hate the fat when people look with,
"she could be attractive if she'd lose
some weight" in their unshielded eyes.

I hate the hopeless battle against fat,
since exercise is isometrically possible,
but not all-out, aerobic effort, or my
back will break again, with months in bed,
and morning consists of an hour willing
myself to rise already, with fat
pressing down and against me.

I hate the fat when it requires
selection of food to be careful,
watchful, against ingesting deadly fat
and being not a meal, but a war of wits
against a conspiracy to make me rounder.

I hate the struggle or the need
to battle against the fat,
but face myself repulsive,
if I lose this war.

    Ursula T. Gibson, 2001

(The reader may be pleased to know this poem helped me
lose 120 pounds in one year).

## LONELY VOICES

From East to West and North to South,
I hear the lonesome voices.
"Where is the one I'll truly love?"
"Why can't I make intelligent choices?"
"Who will understand me?"
"What must I do to find my love?"
"When will it happen? How long must I wait?"

Within me, the sorrow does move me
to tears. What have we done,
in downgrading education
with permissive nonguidance
to create such an unfocused nation
of loneliness? What have we done
in adulation of football shoulders
and cheerleader virtues, to our youth?
What terrible, insurmountable boulders
have we erected, so they can't find
each other, love each other, and dare to be
intelligent, humorous, sharing and caring,
communicative, tolerant, loving, and free?

I explore my heart for answers
and bravely brush away my tears.
I waited thirty-eight years to know my love,
spent many dreadfully lonely years.
I hear the plaintive lonesome voices
from East Coast to the West.
"Keep searching, please; you'll find
that loving one who suits you best."

Ursula T. Gibson 6-10-88

# THE NIGHT I WAS GOING TO KILL MYSELF

When I was very sixteen,
my life was over, wrong, and
to be ended. No one loved me,
no one cared. I knew it always
would be so, because I was myself,
and that was an impossibility.

I drove to the mother sea at night,
half-moon glistening on rolling waves,
silence so strong I could feel my pulse
match the sliding surf, brushing the sand,
and I looked out on ending, on infinity,
only half an hour to exhaustion away.

Ankle-deep in foam, warm summer water
dancing in the moonlight, gray-black waves
beckoning me to plunge and swim,
I looked down and saw phosphorescence—
millions of diatoms fluorescing in the sea,
the smallest life, shining brightly right at me!

I watched the waves around me; every one
was smiling with its native life and light!
"If life so tiny can shine so well,
must I, the larger, try to shine a little?"
I watched and thought, and pain receded
with the ebbing tide. I would go on.

## A Siamese Kitten Contemplates a Mystery

I sit in this white, empty tub.
At one end there is nothing to prance about,
though the shower curtain provides
some possibilities for excitement.

But at this end, a silver pipe sticks out of the wall,
and under it is a deep, dark hole.
I have been brave and reached down that hole with my paw.
There is nothing there to capture.

Suddenly, a drop of water leaps from the pipe,
falls into the hole and is gone!
I saw it fall! I know it fell, but that was so quick,
I must remind myself that it truly happened.

I sniff the hole, look down it again,
but the water drop is gone into the dark.
It is a hole, and water goes down it.
That is its meaning and its life.

I look up at the pipe and see—how interesting! –
another drop of water forming, bigger, bigger,
and suddenly it falls! Down the hole it goes,
just like the other.

Could I have saved it? If I stand just under the pipe,
would the drop of water escape the downness of the hole?
I reach up to the mouth of the pipe
where another forming drop gleams,
and I pat it with my white paw.                              >>

21

The wetness is cold and spreads in the fur between my paw pads.
I shake my paw to free the drop, but it clings desperately.
I lick my paw, removing the water.
Was that better than falling down that deep black hole
in the bottom of this white bathroom tub?
Did my intervention give the drop a meaning to its short life?
Another drop is forming, and helplessly,
I watch it fall down the hole, its life cycle so brief
that if I look away, it has come and gone again.

Why do the water drops form?
Where do they come from?
Does water always fall down holes?
Why do the drops fall down *this* hole?
Must it be that way, every time?
Why do they reject freedom
when it is offered?
Why is life too short
to figure it all out?

Ursula T. Gibson, 2-12-98

22

## The Blossoms of the Night-Blooming Cereus

In weeks, the pimple of green on the side of the stem
grows outward, bends as the blossom head expands,
encased in its brachts, swelling day by day,
'til the tip whitens, the growth attains its goal.

That evening, the blossom unfurls, pressing sepals down,
revealing slender petals of cream
and pistils like fairy's hair,
a bold stamen asserting its power in the middle of them.
In two short hours, the blossom reaches its fullst extent,
eight inches wide of loveliness, exquisite in the darkness
against the tall greenery, awaiting the moth to fertilize.

It blooms all night, this creamy creation,
but in dawn's first light
the flower folds and fades,
the brachts close over it again;
in two short days, the flower that was
is necrotic, black, and falls.
Left behind is nub that may become fruit.
It depends on the success of the insects.

I am not like the night-blooming cereus.
I cannot force my energy and love
into one magnificent display.
My blooming takes years, and
my fruiting takes decades,
and my life lasts many nights
in which no response to my being occurs. >>

I may need to wait for an inner light
or an outer force
before I can reach fruition,
but I *will* grow and *will* open my petals
of mind and heart
and *will* expose myself to possible rejection
or being overlooked,

because staying closed up, unblooming
defeats the purpose of life,
would make me wither before I've lived,
like the night-blooming cereus.

Ursula T. Gibson

## Last One Standing
(tag subject by Bud Silver)

Two years ago, there were
more than a hundred Ponderosa pines
just around the bend, up the road
in the high hills. A hundred pines
reaching their fingers to brush
the moderate clouds that visited
the high hills with lightning
and thunder once or twice a year.

It took just a little beetle,
brown and ugly, to kill
seventy-five of those trees
in less than a year;
it took a wildfire
red and roaring, to kill
twenty of those trees, last year,
so the last ones standing
seem naked in their greenness
in the midst of desolation.

Those last Ponderosa pines
are hope for the future,
if the beetles don't get them
or mankind doesn't light more fires
to kill them. I'd rather sit
under a pine tree with a good book
than anything else called "recreation".
I hope they leave the
last ones standing.

Ursula T. Gibson, 6-04-2004    Revised 6-11-04

## The Elevator

Do you remember your first elevator ride,
when you stepped from a large area into
     a little room?
Doors behind you swished closed,
     and you turned around.
Between adult legs you saw
adult hands pushing buttons on the wall
     and everybody just stood.

Suddenly, a humming sound and
your knees bent, your stomach fell.
A little frightened, you checked
your mother's eyes, and seeing calm,
you bravely waited while your stomach settled.

The doors opened again; everyone walked out.
You were in a different place, another level!
There was the Toy Department, right ahead!
Without hesitation, the miracle of elevators
was accepted. It felt exactly that way
the wonderful day when first you and I met.

Ursula T. Gibson, 1991

## The Chaperone

The Moon was a lovely chaperone.
She hid her face behind a veil of clouds,
And then, you kissed me.
The Moon peeped forth and smiled.

Ursula T. Gibson, circa 1951

## Grand Canyon

They walked up to the south rim
of the Grand Canyon, tourists
looking out and down at red spectrum
and limestone caps, seeing glint
of carving river a mile down,
and he turned to her and said,
"Is this all there is to it? Let's go!"

"Oh, God," I prayed, "open their eyes and hearts
to know what they are seeing!
Let them know the age
of two-billion-year-old stone exposed,
born in water and upheaval.
Let them admire tenacity of plants
clinging to small heaps of fertile earth
caught in the cracks,
the force of water more patient even
than the rocks to keep cutting,
carving a mile down through centuries,
the interplay of force and friction.
Let them read the catalog of creatures caught
in fossil records for a billion years,
untampered and true!
But most of all, Oh, God!
let them know how much
You love this earth
to start the natural process
of which they are a part,
to give us beauty, wonder,
past and future
all within this sight,
this very Grand Canyon!"

But the tourists turned away, car-bound,
and I sorrowed for them, missing it all.

Ursula T. Gibson, October 26, 1990

## Strictly Private

To be so hot in love that I cry out
to live another day! To feel you
near me, on me, oh, so in me
that life's most solid pulsing must be met;
that's what you do with me, in love.

The flowing rush of heat travels with
your searching fingers, and your touch
up and down my body, lightning strokes
emphasized by thunder kisses, cause
ripples of cells striving to meet you,
personal contact so warm and giving
my insides seek to reach you, too, waiting,
pulsing, warming, wetting, needing you.

I breathe barely, small gasps enough to
keep life going; all concentrates the tension
to hold you, to pin myself cell by cell to you,
to let my hips rise to you, my buttocks tighten
to hold you, my legs apart to receive you,
my private self liquid for your pleasure.
Every touch and movement by you stirs response.

Then, power and strength and such great beauty!
Ah, completion, as you enter—that terrible hole
is filled by you as though my other half has found me,
and blood rushes to greet you, and sheer wet joy
makes your entry easy. Welcome! Welcome, Love!

The fire-flame concentrates at hip-level; I can
gasp a breath, consumed by you, one bowed body,
eyes closed now to feel you plunge so deeply,
pulsing, burning rhythm you create, so sought,

surging, 'til I am lifted to the height of it,
straining, giving all to you, open, vulnerable,
only yours, shaking my heart out, passing my life to you.
Ah, take me! take what you will of me, let me give!
Live, seek life, my love; live on in me! Live!
And I'll receive your fire-quenching gift in joy,
overpowering my release with yours, ah, love!

I recover only gradually from athletic strain,
returning from heaven's door to be at your side,
to find you satisfied, accepted, loved, content,
the greatest gift of all. So you give me life.
I rest in your arms, secure and safe, beloved.

Ursula T. Gibson, 1988

## You Lied to Me!

Startled, I've realized you lied to me,
the first time since we met
about such a trivial matter,
but the lying is hard to forget.

You said you were visiting your parents
on Sunday and weren't going to be
in town all weekend. Then why—
can you please explain it—did I see

you, on Sunday, at Lucky's,
carrying packages to your car?
I came over to help you carry,
but you said it wasn't far,

and your eyes shifted leftward and downward.
Your soul's glance would not meet mine.
I knew you knew I knew you'd lied,
and you blushed, not the usual sign

of enjoyment or recognition
that has existed between us two,
but admission of guilt and failure
to do what you knew you should do.

Without explanation, we parted,
and I know I'll never see you again.
Distrust and game-playing don't suit me,
nor does the infliction of pain.

So, learn! my dear friend, what a lie means.
I could handle the truth, whatever it be.
But lies just won't work, not in loving
or building a future. Don't lie to me.

Ursula T. Gibson, 5-29-88

## Couples

In the restaurant, alone,
I tuck myself in a corner,
order, wait, and realize
around me, everyone is
coupled, gazing strong;
close, talking, eyes shining,
together, with chemistry,
sparks echoing stars' insistence,
smiles embracing, voices low and kind.

Oh, lovers, see me not alone,
watching admiringly your
parade of connections.

You speak future together, which
I observe as eagerness, expectation.
You seek to bridge chasms of fear, distrust,
past experience, touching each other's souls
in recognition flickers of cosmic event,
and secret jokes to be yours only.

I love your loving.
It makes the world whole.

Ursula T. Gibson, 08-10-97

## Salt

Chinese mother, when her child
    returns not from Tiananmen Square,
Sheds watered salt the same as

African mother whose child vanishes
    unseen again, for undefined transgressions
    of untribal white laws;  or

Ukrainian mother whose child, expecting
    liberation from Germans, died
    fifty years ago on SS orders;  or

Argentine mother searching for her child
    in dreadful rubble of criminally negligent
    constructions brought down by earthquake;  or

Pakistani mother, hearing gunfire, shouting,
    riot, men's commands, and women's shrieks,
    fears her child's homecoming;  or

Israeli mother, chicken soup helpless,
    waiting for news of the school bus
    her child was riding;  or

Irish mother, wishing the hatred to cease, because
    her child will be next to die, whether
    Protestant or Catholic;  or

Palestine mother who raised her child
    to serve God, hears shots and anger
    from morn to night, and fears God's retaliation;  or    >>

Iranian mother, who once glimpsed freedom
    mourns the child who grew up
    protesting tyranny and died;  or

Scottish mother hugging death fallen from the sky
    on her beloved child because a bomb
    a thousand miles away seemed answer to something;  or

American mother, confronted by kidnap, rape,
    and murder of her child, gang-riddled victim
    of selfish terror, drugs, and personal destruction.

We cry alike for future ended.
We taste the salt our babies were borne in;
tears are the same, the world over.
We women are one, in that.

Ursula T. Gibson, 2-02-02

## Records

(written as an invocation for San Fernando Valley Legal Secretaries
Association on an evening when our speaker was a County Records
official to tell us about recordation rules and fees.)

Birth certificates,
diplomas, degrees,
marriages, divorces,
deeds to homes,
quitclaim deeds,
deaths and burials,
we record our lives' passage.

But the paperwork,
like history itself,
shows only the travel
of the stream,
not the details of life
on the shores.
We keep those unrecorded
in Wills, Trusts, calendars,
poems, notebooks, photos,
postcards, letters, and
the daily hugs, arguments,
resolutions, and smiles
that constitute our real lives.

I hope your records are complete,
abundant, in order, and legible.

Ursula T. Gibson 9-14-99

## Farewell, or How to Say Goodbye Gracefully

Farewell, love of mine.
I must, regrettably, let you go.
Our paths are clearly parting,
even though I love you so.

Farewell, truth of mine,
for what we were, we are no longer.
What might have been has changed,
failing to grow deeper, stronger.

Farewell, heart of mine.
You must not look so sadly
at lovely moments, joyful times,
when we rushed toward each other gladly.

Farewell, essence of mine.
I have from you gifts so bountiful
of kisses, hugs, tenderness, love
that made my life worthwhile and wonderful.

Farewell, being of mine.
Release me now and smile again.
I'll treasure forever and remember
what we have been, despite our current pain.

Farewell, life of mine.
Now, let me go before tears begin
again and make impossible this farewell,
so that I fail and come back in.

Farewell, love of mine.
Going is the best thing I can do for you.
One last sober look between us,
a smile, a nod. To yourself be true.

Ursula T. Gibson, 6-27-88

## Change of Address

I'd buried you and read your Will,
moved clothes, boxes, bills,
closed apartment door,
turned in the keys and left.

Drove to the Post Office, filled out
white card with black lines.
"Old Address" was easy, but
where are you now?
"In care of" me was blunt,
sealing the truth of death.
'Til then, I'd been efficient,
methodical, my eyes were dry,
but handing in that simple card,
I wept and could not stop.

Ursula T. Gibson, 1988

**George de la Tour's "Magdalene with Skull"**
(Los Angeles County Museum of Art,
permanent collection)

She is caught in golden light
of a single candle, flaming,
glowing on the table, book at hand,
shining on her regret, this simple maid
whose life went wrong
until He touched her heart
and turned her life around
from silks, magnificent colors,
to homespun brown and cream,
to contemplate, not men's strong bodies,
but a skull bespeaking mortal end.
Her stare is wistful, reviewing now
the long path ahead while He is gone,
the unending decision to reject
the worldly for the spiritual peace
He gave her, long ago, like candleflame.

Ursula T. Gibson, 1999

## Surprises

If life were placid, staid, and ordinary,
steady, calm, and unperturbed,
if day's undone excitements lay in
opening refrigerator doors, uncurbed
by diets or modern fashion's dictates;
if our relationships just grew,
taken for granted, never worked on,
the outcome always predictably true;

If daily work had no mind-bending challenge,
and everything, even filing, properly flowed,
no problems, no conflicts, no agony to speak of,
and we reaped all just rewards we had hoed,

We would be bored, bored stiff in a minute,
'Cause life's little problems help us win it!

Ursula T. Gibson, June 9, 1998

## Contemplating My Death

One day, I won't be hearing
mockingbirds cascading love
or titmice flitting in scattered chirps
through elm and oak trees,
or sharing Mozart, Schubert, Brahms with you
in quiet enjoyment of perfection.

One day, I won't be savoring
lemon-braised chicken, spaghetti Alfredo,
sweet-covered peanuts, or
your coffee-flavored tongue in love.

One day I won't be seeing
pine trees, quiet lakes, green hills,
the glorious starlit skies, guided by you
to see entirely what is there,
or you, walking up the path to home.

One day, I won't be hugging you,
touching you awake, stroking you to sleep,
knowing you from toe to hair crown,
each lithe muscle, strong bone,
sensitive nerve of you.

One day, I'll die; I can't imagine
anywhere without you, any reason to be
anywhere without you; so I'll vanish
into the Universe's immensity until
we find each other in some form, some way,
some being, some space-time. Any other
concept of dying would be death, indeed.

Ursula T. Gibson, 1997

# The Synthesis of Music,
## a poetic opinionated essay

For the twentieth century, musicians explored
what sound can do. They abandoned
Richard Strauss's extravagant melodies
and romantic glow. Stravinsky and
Shostakovich tore apart consonance,
striving for higher tension and non-relief.
Shoenberg undertook arbitrary order,
forgetting melody except by accident.
Bela Bartok screeched his way to fame.
Aaron Copland preferred dissonance to resolution,
and Lukas Foss played with the tones
of the symphony as though the strings,
winds, brasses, percussion, were
their own individual creations, lacking
conductor or governor over extravagance,
forgetting artistic proportion.
The modern orchestra sounds as though
it were tuning up. I can play that well.

I listen to Phillip Glass's music, most modern,
widely accepted as remarkable, brilliant, new.
I find it repetitive, boring, going nowhere,
imitating thoughts long ago created by masters
and pretending his are different and fresh.
Adding noise to tone fails utterly to move me,
like the ill effect, if dabs of chartreuse paint
were added to brighten the Mona Lisa's smile.
I feel, somehow, dirty inside, listening to Glass,
as though my inner purity had been defiled
and a musical rape against my will had occurred.

Repetitive bass, passacaglia ground with no spirit,
dull thumps of low notes, swimming upper range
rattling on and on with no resolution, no relief,
fake counterpoint disregarding all the magic
of one set of notes played against another set.
All of this, praised as New Wave, New Sound, Neo-Modern,
is not the synthesis of Classic, Romantic, and
Modern Schools of composition I hoped for.

The "trickle down" of such effects into
popular music has occupied half a century,
getting louder, not deeper; getting sexy,
not more intense; drowning feelings, not
heightening them; cheapening human values,
not exploring human capability to be true.
Those like Carl Orff or Ernest Bloch who
wrote for the spirit were drowned out by noise.

What will music be in the Twenty-First Century?
We have a new beginning again to make music
rise from the heart, tempered by good judgment,
communicating melody, harmony, tone, rhythm,
not merely sex, violence, fear, anxiety, noise,
but what the noble human being is, what we can be.
Music that fails to move the human spirit
fails in its ultimate purpose: to give us
a glimpse of immortality, of lasting love.

Modern music fails to do that; it has been
intellectualized into oblivion.
I'll keep my Mozart, Beethoven, Schubert,
Brahms, Mendelsohn, Verdi, Offenbach,
Schumann, Johann Strauss
and Richard Strauss recordings on hand
to turn to when I need to be lifted
beyond my temporal state to the sublime.

Ursula T. Gibson, 2001

## Laws Meant to Be Broken

Your touch is warm and gentle;
you tell me I feel warm to you.
We break the laws of physics—
one of us ought to be cooler.

Your eyes meet mine; I melt.
My eyes meet yours; you burn.
We break the laws of physics—
Two heats melting each other!

I see you shine so brightly;
you say you reflect my light.
We break the laws of physics—
Two suns, two planets, side by side.

You hold me close and breathless;
I hold you near and blend with you.
We break the laws of physics—
Two beings occupying the same space and time.

Ursula T. Gibson 7-24-88

## Why Should I Cry?
### (In Memory of Rudolf L. Shouldice, my son, December 1, 1953, to April 11, 2000).

He is no longer here on Earth
in form my eyes can see,
where he was captured since his birth.
Now he again flies free.

He need not struggle against gravity
nor search for love, nor fear
the coming night, nor mankind's cruelty.
Why should I cry, now he is there?

The universe is his to find;
the answers to his honest query
rest open for his spirit mind
to dwell in perfect harmony.

There is a promise at this time of year
that we will be together once again;
in certainty that dispels fear,
I await that hour, release from pain.

The days we spent together are not gone,
as I remember him. His smile and eager flight
will welcome me when I go home.
Why should I cry, when all will be made right?

Ursula T. Gibson, © 4-20-02

## Neighborhood Announcements

Around the block, I hear
the Rottweiler bellow his objections,
and two doors west of his mansion,
the happy Beagle trumpets to oppose movement
on territory he considers quite his own.
At the pink house around the block,
the terrier-mix rattles his chains
and yaps snappy protests,
followed by the Great Dane's
deep woofs woven with threatening grunts
and crashes against the chain link fence
in the large back yard of the house
with the blue chimney.

Those dogs grow quiet as progress
is made past the cottage with five cats
and the pot-bellied pig's home,
but the moment the pit bull terrier
at the west end of our block sees him,
the raucous rage of five dogs
up the street west of our house begins.
Two chihuahuas chime in yapping;
a Scottish terrier yelps and snarls;
a collie growls and races back and forth,
only quieting as the irritant passes on.
The dogs quiet down, satisfied.
They have again succeeded in
driving off the intruder from their
territory, their guarded homes.

I open my door to greet the mailman.

Ursula T. Gibson, © 4-27-2000

## Earthturning

Earthturning inevitably hides the setting sun.
In twenty minutes, that glorious light is gone,
Remaining golden rays caught gleaming in the mist,
Allowing glints of daylight which may long persist.
Eastward, the purple terminator arcs to sea
To let the shadowed mountains rest dreamily.

The quiet night approaches, but my heart
Will find no peace while we're apart.
I feel the earthturn bring us closer, yet
These hours apart are time I can't forget,
The space between us, vast as heaven's dome;
I long to be with you, my real home.

There, in the East, a faint star's early light
Reminds me still that this is just one night.

Ursula T. Gibson, 4-18-89


## Hurt

Wounds need attention,
sooner or late;
Hurts need comfort and
love, not hate.

Ursula T. Gibson, July 5, 1988

## I'll Never Ask

I'll never ask
if you love me as much
as I love you.

Love is not measurable
like cupsful of sugar
or teaspoonsful of
vanilla extract.

If you love me,
the quantity is not the issue;
quality is what matters:
the way you look at me,
kindnesses you have given me,
the courage to live you supply,
the touch of your hand
when I put mine within reach,
the happy tone of your voice
when you call out,
"I'm home!"
and generous kisses
that make my heart beat faster
and my knees weak.

I'll never ask.
I know.

Ursula T. Gibson, 12-11-03

## The Blue Blanket

We offer you this blue wedding gift
to share with you the love we found
and dream with you the splendor of your future.
We know your new Blue Blanket will shelter you
as our own wedding gift Blue Blanket,
now thirty-six years old, has favored us.
This Blue Blanket may grow antique with you,
a soft repository of your memories together.

This Blue Blanket's serene hue is cloudless, calm.
Under its folds, your togetherness finds shelter.
It's an umbrella to keep the storms of life at bay.
Keep it dry and cozy, warm and safe;
don't let disputes dampen it, worries wrinkle it.
Spend time together; talk arguments out, find
reasonable answers in the living room
before you snuggle together in the Blanket's warmth.

This Blue Blanket means sharing your bed
and leaving space for breathing, but
hugs and love are woven in its threads.
Use them as needed; give them any time.
This Blue Blanket is winterweight, but washable;
troubles that seem large are washable, too.
The deep, good humor by which you enjoy
each other is, blanket-like, widespread.

This Blue Blanket can last your lifetimes,
given care and attention, cleaning and pride.
Expansion to include familial satellites
is not beyond its capacity; blankets like kids.
This Blue Blanket, winter and summer, will
unite you, symbolize, as you slip to sleep,
your individual wholeness now made one;
keeping you warm and safe for the morning.

This Blue Blanket belongs to both of you.
You can pull it this way and that; it will
remain whole and flexible as you grow together,
stretching yourselves to embrace all of life.
This Blue Blanket is your repose together;
snuggle often in its warmth; love each other,
so you can pass Blue Blanketness on
to those who follow, just as we have done.

Ursula T. Gibson, © 1990

## Hiatus

At times, I feel the poems are done,
    And no more singing will occur.
    I feel disconnected from everyone,
        And life becomes a misty blur.

The routine things that I can do
    Make time pass in a meaningless way,
        While disparate words fail to unite, and
        Significant ideas continue to stray.

But then, the key in our front door
    Announces your return to home,
        And like lightning, like rainstorm,
            Like sunrise and joy, the poems come.

Ursula T. Gibson, 10-14-88

## Babies

"Oh, he's beautiful!" the women say.
"Just look at him!" they say,
voices tender with acceptance,
gathered around the newborn.
"Just look at her!" the women say,
sweetening pronunciation.
"Isn't she adorable!" they say.
The men stand 'round, awed a little
by newborn tininess and perfection.
They pass out symbols of achievement,
cigars, though they don't smoke,
flowers, handshakes and congratulations,
to make themselves part of newness,
part of life's continuation.

Acceptance of babies has nothing
at all to do with facts. The baby
may have birth-red, wrinkled skin,
a screwed-up face with puckered lips,
eyes resisting the work of light,
tight fists, baby pudge or
baby scrawn, no hair or lots of it,
and a Herculean voice protesting living.
Whatever. None of that matters.
A baby remains utterly lovely.

What do we see in beginning life
that urges exclamation?
"What use is a newborn baby," Churchill said.
Do we love all babies,
hope encapsulated in helplessness?                    >>

We, from our vantage of choices made
and choices removed from our own lives,
imagine all the choices this new life
still has: potential to be realized,
talent to be discovered, ability to be
fostered, mind to be made aware,
love to be created, care to be given,
mistakes to be avoided,
courage to be admired,
independence to be achieved,
roads to be traveled, stretching
around the universe.

"Oh, isn't he beautiful!"
"Oh, isn't she adorable!"

Ursula T. Gibson, 10-22-90

**Serene Moments**
**(a list poem)**

When I can see the horizon;
wind stops blowing;
the lights turn off.
The moon slips below the edge of earth,
letting stars show their power.

When I learn an unfamiliar flower's name;
a bird cascades music;
the lake laps a little at the shore;
you come into the room.

When the kitten purrs;
joyful eyes meet,
friends hug;
the fire turns to gentle embers;
the baby falls asleep;
you hold me.

Ursula T. Gibson, © 6-20-2000

## Crescent Moon

The thinnest moon crescent
when first light reflects from the limb
and trembles yellow-white in the blue-black night
rarely is noticed. We see full moons.

So I, a sliver crescent in your life
accept myself reflecting your light,
unnoticeable in the blue vault of your being.
Full moon is unattainable.
In the dark blue night, my candlepower
of light can shine as well;
all that must happen in the focus
of your eyes to see me.

Ursula T. Gibson, © 7-13-888

## The Easy Lay

The word went out on campus:
"She's an easy lay; just take her out to dinner,
tell her she's pretty, and you need her."
She was a musician, so of course,
she was an easy lay; aren't all musicians?
"She went through men like a street sweeper,"
they said after three years of higher education.

What they didn't know was, deliberately,
she wasn't playing the American sex game.
She wasn't holding off and teasing;
she wasn't playing carrot-on-a-stick,
or "how much of your life will you pay to get me?"
She didn't accept sex as a goal to be attained,
or denial of sex as woman's ultimate weapon.
She was working her own life plan.

She's decided that sex was natural,
but sex alone wasn't love, not lasting love.
She felt the sexual double-standard was
degrading to both men and women;
that both women and men wanted sex, and
she'd get the sexual challenge out of the way
to see if anything deeper might be possible.
Some relationships were overnight;
others lasted months; a few approached
lovingness and lasted a year or two.                    >>

She never went with more than one man at a time;
in each relationship, she was faithful to her lover.
She was fun in bed and out; she worked hard and
helped her lovers as needed. She made music
and good dinners; she listened to plans and dreams,
frustrations and sorrows, wishes and needs.
She hoped and waited for permanence,
friendship, and combined futures. She gave
her whole intelligent self without hesitation
and took the consequences as they came.

Men taught her a great deal, and she remembered,
but each new acquaintance was his own, unique self.
What others had done or been didn't apply.
As years went on, she kept on hoping that
she'd meet the man who would be honest, too.

When she reached 30, her counsellor raised eyebrows
at a count of 46 men in 11 years.
"So many penises! Why?" the psychologist wondered.
"Somewhere out there," she said, "someone exists
who will see me not merely as large breasts or soft belly,
or hot or easy, in sexual fragments or as an ego tool
to be used that then discarded. Someone will see me
as his life partner, his soulmate, his deepest love."

A few years later, when she married,
that marriage lasted all her life.
This man saw her whole, mind, body, and spirit,
and treasured and nurtured her, as she did him.
They made love 'til they died in their 80s,
all sorts of love from pillow fights to
last-gasp private orgies, from eyes meeting
across a room and handholding in the movies,
from savageness to tenderness and back again;
parenting love and post-parenting love, and
hours-long political and philosophical discussions,
and love in music, love in art, love in literature,
love in nature, love in excellence of human striving,
love in work, and love in play,
all framed in love; all, two humans united.

Which is the kind of woman that all those guys
who took her sex and threw it away as cheap
or weren't ready to commit to a depth relationship,
or were afraid they'd have to be more than penis power,
had been looking for, all along.

Ursula T. Gibson, 1990

## The Generic Life

She lived a generic life—
like toothpaste and aspirin instead of
Crest and Tylenol,
like car, not Cadillac;
school, graduation, college,
all framed in generic Chevies;
movies to make her laugh or cry,
generic meals with generic dates,
various generic jobs like
McDonald's and Wal-Mart;
romantic love, serious love,
nights of half-moonlight,
days of hazy sunshine;

and a wedding with generic maid-of-honor,
best man, bride's maids,
crying mother, stoic father,
and even an attentive groom;

generic apartment with one bedroom;
generic apartment with two bedrooms;
house with mortgage and three bedrooms,
and four generic children who
generically crawled, walked, climbed,
ran, pestered, spent money on
toys, books, clothes, computers,
bikes, cars, girls, boys.

As she watched her generic life unfold,
she questioned, infrequently,
whether this was all there was.
She shared her simple concerns with
generic women friends over cups of tea
(not Herbal or Lipton or International),
cooked thousands of generically healthy meals

for her family, read novels at bedtime,
joined the local "Y" for exercise.
The moments of joy and pain that
punctuated her generically average existence
were, actually, average joys and pains,
with no heart-rending, soul-breaking,
mind-bending heights or depths.
But such fleeting inquiries into
the generic state of things didn't last long.
She drifted through the generic platitudes
of her life, finally drifting
comfortably to ultimate sleep in bed,

never knowing the soul-stirring strains
of Brahms and Mozart, or
the miracle of height of a Sequoia tree,
depth of the Grand Canyon,
white marble of Florence,
cathedrals of Europe and Washington, D.C.,
red sandstone of Colorado,
bird song in Connecticut forests,
rolling Mississippi at New Orleans,
the Columbia Gorge's breadth and
its surprising waterfalls,
the rippling of hot air over Mojave Desert,
the aroma of sweet meats over an open fire,
the intimate snuffling of horses hobbled at night,
winding roads to astronomical observatories,
traveling planets, glowing comets,
shadows on white walls by Venus light,
wheeling galaxies, a glimpse of eternity,
all just within the sight of God.

Ursula T. Gibson, 1990

## Why Lovers Are Blind

It wasn't the day's sun
or the night's white moon.
It wasn't a flashlight or headlight,
a lightning flash or a search beam.
It was the light in your deep eyes,
the vigor of your presence,
the beauty of your words,
the hope you gave my heart,
and I was left comfortably blinded.

Ursula T. Gibson, 11-13-03

## Elderly Protest Against Spring at 6:00 A.M.

Dear God, why do you keep waking me up
so early? The morning sun touches my eyes,
and I drown in a flood of mockingbird song.
Spring smells of purple jacaranda and orchid trees,
thick honey in the air, and manicured mowed grass
welcoming laughing children noisily living,
with joy and wonder crashing through my window.

Let me sleep through it all; it's time to
rest forever, so God, in mercy, please,
turn off your glorious alarm clocks.

Ursula T. Gibson, 11-17-90.

## Dachau

I cannot rise above the haunting eyes
staring and weeping in this century.
    Before me, foundations mark outlines,
    barracks where they were stowed and died.
        I see grey gravel, muddy earth,
        hushed voices, too many tears.

I sit on a bench in green memorial Dachau;
but for the grace of courage, accident, God,
    my father, mother, brother, and I
    would form its remaining ash heaps,
        clang of its crematoria doors
        would have closed behind me, too.

Now, green grass grows where groveled
"political Enemies of the State" in system
    forbidding thought. They died; grass cannot hide
    ghosts that rise, the whisper of voices
        rustling in the trees, around the walls;
        no sod can bury despair and truth forever.

I cannot rise above the haunting eyes;
they see me now; I will not escape
    from solemn connection to terribleness
    that happened here, and what again will be
        if we fail to remember the cost of freedom;
        if we fail to remember.

Ursula T. Gibson, May 19, 1989

## Time to Wait

Oh, when we're young, we have time to wait!
We can wait to see how things turn out;
we can wait to see who's important or popular;
we can wait to learn the subjects they throw at us;
we can wait to find that one friend, that one confidant
with whom our youth will be shared forever.

But when we're old, we have no time to wait.
Everything must be lived today; the answers must be true;
we don't need popularity, but longevity.
And if we haven't learned what we need by now,
we never will. Our friends are lifetime friends
who have been through our life experiences with us,
the two or three who have lived as long as we have.
The time to wait is almost over. Then, let's see
what we've really been waiting for: what comes next.

Ursula T. Gibson, 10-01-03

# To My Astronomer Husband
# (James Gibson, b. 6-9-28)

See all these poems I've written?
Most of them are about you.
Oh, I try to enlarge them, make them
fit the universe and other people,
touch the general humanity, say
something meaningful, and elicit
common feelings and experience,
but they're really all you.

I write about an evening sky;
between the lines you lead me to
fifteen billion light years and
jewelry in gaseous form,
to comets and minor planets traveling
in a gently-moving, cataclysmic cosmos
of unanswered questions,
where nothing stays the same, and
the observation not made is lost forever.

I write about lovers and loving;
between the lines, your tenderness
and wonder at our meeting, and
all the marvelous things we've done,
all efforts we've made to understand,
and my life shines because of
your aware love, persistent love,
faithful love, passionate love,
friendship love, lasting love.

I write about pain, despair, fear;
between the lines, you're coaxing me
back to life, ability, courage,
to a highway I can walk again; and
your filling the gaps, doing the work
I cannot do, plunging in when I need
something done or when I need you,
makes pain, despair, fear, writeable.

I write about my past, my lonely past;
between the lines, your soul contact
removes loneliness and enables me to
investigate its roots. I could not
venture into such fearful ground
without your arm about my shoulders,
your smile and voice at my ear,
your patience as I blunder in the dark.

I write about experiences, events;
between the lines, your steady path
of honesty, direction, integrity,
colors all experience from our fortress
we have built together. That I'm in love
is obvious to all who read my poems;
that you are my beloved should be
self-evident in all they read.

See all these poems I've written?
Most of them are because of you.

Ursula T. Gibson, 6-21-90

## My Child

You were born;
your tiny fingernails etched my heart;
your delicate hands entwined my own;
your healthy voice imprinted on my ear;
your robust body fit my arms;
your hungry mouth gained nourishment from me;
your wonderful eyes caught my soul;
and I was yours for life.

Ursula T. Gibson, 8-4-89

## Motherhood

We will raise voyagers to the Moon, Mars, Io, Ganymede,
or wanderers among weighty words to heighten love and peace.
We will grow courageous hearts saying "No!" to war, to drugs,
to lowliness and self-effacement, instead to do great deeds.
We will generate the workers and doers, the conscientious,
the contributors, the decent people of next generation;
We will treasure personal freedom, honor country's worth,
in not one-sided consideration of the present and the future;
we will foster feeling persons, not ashamed to cry at death
or when the heart flows over joyfully, tear-bright laughter.

We will guide and scold and praise and lead; we will help them
to discover their own future, to see their contributions.
We will listen to hours of discovery, pain, excitement,
worry, hope, fear, and striving, calmly reassuring them.
We will paint possible dreams for them to dream, and
proudly watch their own dreams forming and attained.
We will open doors for their minds and provide steps
for their hearts and souls to climb far beyond our own.
We will hope and think and plan and scrape money together
as needed to give them that one more step toward light.

We will not eat lunch so *they* can have nourishment;
we will not buy our new dress so *they* can look presentable;
we will not go to movies so they can gather, laugh or cry.
We will urge them through high school and cry at graduation;
we will help them to college and cry at resulting adulthood;
we will watch them love and marry, or not marry,
bear children or live in solitary creativity, work or
not work, rise or not rise, and we will laugh and cry.
We will encourage human beings, "Be yourself, you, unique,
and add your gifts and light to this dreary world."

When all that we will do is done, they will not know it all.
Our gratifying end is a telephone call: "Hi, Mom!"

Ursula T. Gibson, July 1989

# My Mother's Grave
## (a tribute to Gabriele Winkler Schindler, 12-1-1898 to 3-11-1964)

My mother lives not in this cold plot of ground
where flowers wilt in a day or two and grass grows,

but when my husband calls, "Where are my glasses?"
and I find them, not having seen him take them off;
or when I become aware enough to fix the hurts or
soothe ruffled tempers, like my mother did
on hot summer days when we tumbled off our bikes;
or when I hold my breath and withhold words
that never should be spoken, as my mother did
in kindness and concern for others' feelings;
or when my family grunts in satisfaction
for a meal well cooked; or when I hear
the favored key opening my door, and I welcome you
with smile and kiss, unpainting the day's troubles.

Then, my mother lives.

Ursula T. Gibson, 7-16-89

## The End of the Long Sentence

Funerals are for the living
to say goodbye,
to sort the memories,
to put to rest the quarrels,
the arguments, the differences,
to stop the flow of communication,
to end the pain,
to sigh with relief
that the beloved
is safe, loved, and eternal.

Funerals are not for those who died.
They have realized their reward
for living in this dear Earth.
A funeral is for the living,
the final period
to the long sentence of life.

Ursula T. Gibson, Copyright 5-5-04

## A Slight Difference

A bud rising from a bush of leaves
stretches its stem and searches the sun.
It folds back sepals, lets a petal down.
The silken velvet offers its beauty
as the flower finds its strength.
Its color fills the eyes;
its scent reminds us of perfection
as the rose gives itself to us.

We are all roses waiting to burst
from buds on tall stems of learning,
opening ourselves to sunlight of expertise,
to spread our colors of courage
and perfume of perfection.

The difference between a rose and us
is that the flower must wait
for sunlight, food, and water,
but we can bloom at will,
because we can make it happen.

Ursula T. Gibson, June 13, 2000
(Invocation for SFVLSA meeting)

## Bikers

A century ago or more, they
would have ridden horses
wildly in and out of town,
guns snapping, boots thumping
ribs of straining mustangs,
roaming prairies
out to freedom.

Now, their steeds are two-wheeled,
roaring half-tipped up and down city streets,
responsive to hands and weight, not heels,
bandannas grasping waving hair against the wind,
slashing up mountains into hiding,
out of sight.

Ursula T. Gibson, July 24, 1989.

## Reasons to Cry

"Your wife left with another man,"
the neighbor explained,
and the strong man cried.

"The street drugs will surely kill you,"
the doctor frowned,
and the strong man cried.

"You drink too much; your job is gone,"
his boss, his friend, announced,
and the strong man cried.

"You haven't paid; can't borrow more,"
his loan shark smirked,
and the strong man cried.

"Your child is dead,"
the policeman said,
and the strong man cried.

"The accident was your fault,"
the judge pronounced,
and the strong man cried.

"God loves you; **help** yourself!"
the angel smiled,
and the strong man cried.

Ursula T. Gibson, © 7-7-00

## Sit and Wait

"I'm tired. I don't know what to do,"
I told my mother, one long afternoon.
"Sit still and wait for ten minutes;
see what happens; watch what wanders by."
I sank down beside her on the park grass,
blue sky with dots of white clouds overhead,
brightened by slanting afternoon sunlight.

In the green grass with square-cut blades
that showed the mowing patterns,
a line of ants, coming and going,
(with individuals stopping,
touching feelers,
and wandering on)
passed a stand of leafy dandelions
(the lion's tooth plant),
which adroitly had bent under
the mower's blades and lived.
My eyes roved up the blossoming stems,
where two ladybugs displayed
their bright red wing covers
with seven black polkadots
in fashionable array.
To the top of the bare flower stem,
each bug struggled, arranging
its tiny six legs carefully
as the breeze blew against the flower,
and at the top, in deliberate,
methodical ceremony,
uncapped the filamentary, dainty wings,
and flew!                                        >>

No sooner were they gone than a great,
rust-brown horned beetle stumbled by,
tipping, rocking, mounting obstacles
of pebbles, sliding up and down
the sand pits left by earthworms
and salpugids, taking two steps
forward and one step back
(like some people do). It took a while,
but he reached his burrow in the side
of the hill ten feet away.
Next to that, a trapdoor spider's home
remained mysteriously shut;
the deceptive web well hidden
by leaves and earth,
cleverly interwoven.

Suddenly, a song burst clear upon the air!
We sat quite still and listened.
A bird—a robin—descended from his elm tree perch;
I heard his wings, he flew so close to me,
to hop, hop, hop and listen; hop, hop, hop, and listen.
He made sudden, stabbing forays into the grass.
At last, with wiggling worm securely skewered
and hauled into the daylight,
the red-breasted carnivore departed in a whirr of air.

I felt quite earth-connected now.
The living I had seen in ten minutes of stillness
would remind me all my years that life goes on,
no matter how tired or lonely,
how isolated or sad,
how bereft of beauty,
or weary of mankind's meanness I might be.
I looked at my mother with newfound wisdom.
She smiled. "It's time to go home," she gently said.
But I picked a dandelion,
and pressed it between the pages
of the five-pound dictionary in my room.

Ursula T. Gibson 11-11-88

## Upset

After dinner and the movie,
we entered the night,
my new-found man and I.
He worked at an observatory,
studying stars. I was merely
a secretary, but when I saw that
open sky with full Moon clinging
to treetops, I thought I knew
his major love.

"Oh, what a beautiful sky!
Look at the light in the treetops,
and the Moon, so large and golden!"
I waited for his response.

"The enemy," he stated.

"The enemy?" I puzzled.

"I can't observe the stars
when the Moon is full.
Its light defeats incoming emissions
of light from stars and comets,
or reflections from moving asteroids
whizzing by. It's called 'bright run,'
and faint star observers have
a few nights off."

What an upset of all romantic Moon symbolism
taught to me since childhood!
The Moon, uninspiring, dreamless, loveless,
to be wished away so my man's joy in work
could be untroubled!

Once a month, when the Moon is full,
dominating the heavens,
my star observer grumps and mutters
in the face of the "enemy,"
but I smile, because he's home!

Ursula T. Gibson, 9-21-01; revised 3-12-04

## Winter Sky

Oh, Orion, sword on belt,
   with hidden, star-forming nebula jewel-gleaming,
   transparent black velvet around Betelgeuse,
   ruby-red brooch at your shoulder,
and Sirius, trailing puppy blue-bright at your heels,
stretch me to your side!
   We'll stroll the heavens to sight Andromeda's Galaxy,
   Two million, four hundred thousand years of travel
for the light we see from her this moment!
I am so small! That's true.
But I'm the observer!

Ursula T. Gibson, 12-27-88

## Experience

I've never worked in a factory,
    but I can hear in my mind's ears
the clanging, banging, shuddering noise,
the whistling, gristling, musclebound noise.

I've never worked on a trawler,
    but I can feel in my mind's arms
the tossing, bossing, surging sea,
the slapping, clapping, netbound sea.

I've never worked in a coal mine,
    but I can sense in my mind's hands
the thundering, blundering resisting ore,
the sweating, wetting earthbound ore.

I've never worked in a space shuttle,
    but I can see in my mind's eye,
the pushup, whoosh-up, escaping roar,
the silent, tranquillent, spacebound roar.

I've never worked a lot of places,
    but I can taste in my mind's tongue
the salty, weighty, rapturous adventures,
the gentle, mental, lifebound adventures.

I've worked in offices, with people around,
    but I can feel in my mind's heart
the far-flung, star-hung, astronomical spaces,
the yearning, burning, starbound spaces.

Ursula T. Gibson, 1996

**Warm Snow**
**(tag topic by Death Here 2)**

The blustery night
that left our windows frosted
and our toes cold when they touched
the floors, faded in blasts of wind
that trickled to mere breezes,
as the winter sun struggled above the horizon
and spread some feeble light.
But the snowclad roads and sidewalks,
the garden path, the hills around us
glowed in rising sunlight like golden fields,
with tendrils of Spring on its way, and warm snow.

Ursula T. Gibson 7-3-04

## DISTANCES

How far can I think?
Geometrically, from Earth's sharp orbit
to the Sun, our closest star;
by parallax to nearby stars and clusters;
by comparison of Cepheid variables' luminosity
to distant clusters throughout our Galaxy,
and bursting the confines of the Milky Way,
by resolution of stars in Andromeda,
to two million, four hundred thousand light years!

Next, the determination of how far our Local Group
of slowly-turning galaxies was spead
in space and time; and discovery of discord
in those distances compared to other Island Universes
which hang so tantalizingly in our sky,
but travel away from us in all directions, outward,
existing from ten million light years
into all of space-time.

Then, by galactic redshifts, far away
to galaxies and clusters of hundreds of galaxies
not in our Local Group, with the eye
of the Five Meter Telescope or
the Hubble Space Telescope to a billion light years!
And discerning quasars and the lumpy universe,
combined with radio wave observations,
stretching my mind's eye to fifteen billion
light years—the youth of our Universe!

That's how far, how old I can think.
But the distance and wisdom of your eyes
cause me even more wonder.

Ursula T. Gibson, 6-5-88; rev. 8-13-04

## A Charlet Sequence
(A Charlet is a syllabic poem, 6,6,9,2
invented by Charlotte Bridges, Alaska)

Rosy-faced, tight-petaled
Palomar sweetpeas bloom,
climbing my fence because I stole seeds
for me.

Red-faced flax, dark centers
shining graceful in sun,
dainty borders, bringing Cordoba
to me.

Mexican salvia,
Purple spikes so easy-tall,
lure hummingbirds to flit my garden
near me.

Pleasant memories of
special places where my
garden flowers first were met and loved
by me.

Mountaintop and desert,
veld and rolling hilltops,
Argentina, Africa, so far
from me.

Ursula T. Gibson, 2001

## Oak Tree Down
## (written the same day Sammy Davis, Jr. and
## Jim Henson both died— 5-16-1990).

The sheltering oak tree died this week,
its damaged base abandoning the ground
when rain-heavy branches jerked loose its roots
and tilted it beyond gravity. The sad sight
of armillaria-rotted stump, leaning air-exposed,
shrieked pain, as though the wood were crying.

The gray squirrel views the fallen oak,
accepting loss with squirrely shoulder-shrug
and tail flick to hop across the roof
to other trees. A blue jay lights
on tilted branch and squawks a puzzled protest.
Mockingbird spreads white-rimmed wings
to leave her perch, her nesting tree,
her usual home.

No more raccoon trundling
across our roof to feast on ripening acorns,
snorting pleasure amid the oak leaves,
squeaking messages to his kinfolk a block away.
The oppossum cannot hide from sun and people there,
and titmice must cavort in other branches.
A patch of sky that had been greenery a week ago
now is daylight, sunshine blue and shadeless.

Suddenly, the neighbor's fence and roof
are visible; the oak tree is down and gone.
It left its beauty only in our memory.
The world is different for us now.

Ursula T. Gibson, 5-16-90; rev. 4-12-93

## Avalanche

When life's rudeness
overwhelms you,
buries you in dark,
all you can do is
dig upward with
all your might and skill.

After sorrow, pain,
there may be light
to be gained by
digging yourself out!

Ursula T. Gibson, 4-8-98

## Spirited

All right, I'll accept the bit today,
but I might not, tomorrow.
You may cinch the girth and
lengthen stirrups, now,
smoothing saddle blanket down.
But next time, I might
protest and fill my lungs
before the strap grows tight.

This lovely morning
I'll accept your weight
and answer to the reining,
but when I rear or buck, too late
for graceful, hasty dismount,
I'll make it clear the power is mine,
and my consent depends on trust,
before the reins your hands entwine.

Ursula T. Gibson, 8-4-89

(This poem was the Golden Diamond prize winner
-- $100.00 --in MUSE Magazine, Dec. 1989)

## Questions, No Answers
## (an autobiographical inquiry*)

The great sad fear is this:

What I am, what I know, what I've loved
will be lost, not passed on, vanished, when I die.

Who will care for Schubert's songs and cry
for the miller boy who loved so badly?
Do you hear the dogs barking at strangers,
driving the Wanderer away?
Are you convinced of ravens' fidelity?

Who will argue that Don Octavio should never
wield a gun in the first act duel with Don Giovanni,
or that Cherubino may not touch the Countess,
let alone roll in bed with her, but
worships her from afar?
Will others recognize Mozart, Beethoven, Brahms,
and Richard Strauss within three measures?
Where will the perspective on Wagner's ponderosity
ever come from to balance overextended adulation?
Who will read the written music and play for love?
Will someone conduct KUSC music while he's driving
and sing all four voices of the choral music, too?
Who will bask in music as in friendship, and
keep the listening standards high and true?

Will Rembrandt and Ver Meer hold anyone else's attention,
aside from grudging intellectual admiration?
Will Juno be anything except a heavy-set lady
encrusted in jewels? Will others know
the De la Tour "Magdalene," the one with skull, as truth,
instead of Titian's simpering noblewoman
dressed in lavish silks by that same name?
How many will identify the statue "Satan" as
the moment of realization of that fallen angel
that it didn't work out the way he planned?

In Buenos Aires in the Supreme Courthouse plaza,
Justicia, young, lovely, arms outstretched,
stays blind and needs our sightful assistance.
Who sees her there and recognizes the power
of blind Justice reaching for our help?
And San Martin astride his gentle mare gazes
from Cerro de Gloria toward the Andes,
knowing the hard task of freedom
lying before him and his men.

Will others watch the sky for passing clouds
to wish them on their way so astronomers
might ply their craft and science without hindrance?
Who will remember zodiacal light rising
behind the Andes mountains in the west,
or shadows on white building walls
caused by Venus-light in a night so dark
the ginger cat could not be seen, but only heard,
galloping across the pebbled parking lot,
Mrrrping to greet us in the dark.                    >>

Or high peaks aflame in setting sunlight
caught in blowing snow banners?
Or winter mountaintops in moonlight,
suspended, floating above the dark valley
in the midst of the equally dark sky?

Who will know Cape cobra snakes sliding down
the garden path, glistening in the sunlight,
and raising marked hood only to warn me
not to follow so closely. Will anyone talk
with the cats, earnest conversation?
Will the chorisia, the Palo Borracho, the
Kapokbaums, the Floss-silk trees (all the same
species, just different names) continue to bloom?
Will anyone teach the neighborhood children
to like snails and not to scream at spiders,
mice and lizards? How many hawks will sail
unnoticed, or mockingbirds be unheard?

And the fleet horses with their tender mouths—
who will rein them and ride, and who unsaddle
the worthy steed and wash him down?
Amid the pines up the mountain trail,
are there deer and raccoons unseen?
And in rhythm, too, the gray whales wander
up and down the California coast, regularly,
reliably—how long? And who will watch them?

Who will know the joy of natural childbirth,
as I did, in this age of quelling the idea of pain
and undertaking no natural behavior whatsoever?
Who will see the beauty of a child growing
alert and free, curious and interested?
Who will see the world entire, treasuring its unity,
belonging to its rhythm, caring for its preservation,
understanding the eternal process that leads to life?

Does anyone care about our history to make good prevail?
Atrocity was part of my knowledge: Dachau and Hitler
were the thunder of my childhood, to be feared.
We were so very fortunate to find our American home
during that disaster. We must not allow repetitions
in smaller numbers of the philosophy that
one person is entitled to live while another,
dissenting, shall be slaughtered! I resist
tearing down, carving up, disposing of,
but my times now are filled with apathy and terrorism.
The great acts of our times are war, assassination,
destruction, hostages, and recriminations;
whatever happened to "one world," one peace, one aim
to make man free to understand his God?
Such ideas begin at home; stop the bullies
on the playground!

My ethics have governed me ruthlessly;
who else knows them? Who will cross the street
at corner and wait for "walk" lights, and
pay back their employers for stamps used at work?
Will anyone insist that work that is lawful
has its honor, and that if you're paid by the hour,
you do an hour's work?
Would anyone teach the rewards of doing
more than expected?

Will lovingness continue, when I am gone?
There must be others who will transmit
ideas and acts of caring, curiosity, hope, excitement,
reading thousands of books and meeting people earnestly!
Will relationships be built on honesty and trust,
relying not on drugs and artificiality,
but joy in being fully human? I mourn for those
who maim themselves, seeking "highs" drug-borne,                >>

93

instead of elevation by their efforts and creativity.
So unproud are they; so blinded by their habits
that they see not the dull, sick future and the
painful lives they've made, if they should live that long.

What has my life been worth, if no one remembers
or preserves my loves? Has anything I've done
been worth preserving? Whose life has been made better
because I've lived? What have I left to be remembered by?

In college, we asked similar questions as we faced
the fact that we were really responsible for our own lives.
Bull sessions with friends 'til 4:30 a.m. nightly.
Then it was, "What good am I? What can I do?"
"How can we fix it?" "Is there a better way?"

Now it comes down to simpler questions:
"What good have I been? What have I done
which might be considered worthy to last
beyond my own demise?" Same questions,
different times, no answers. Despite a lifetime
of building a fund of living, loving,
worrying and working, just to find a few answers.

Only God knows, and I will have to await
the end of life to know what God might know.

That is the great sad fear.
It's also my greatest hope.

Ursula T. Gibson, 7-13-88; rev. 8-12-04.

\* (with references to actual experiences in
Illinois, California, Connecticut, western Argentina,
central South Africa, and California again).

## PREPARED

Where you will come from, I don't know.
Who you will be remains a mystery.
But one day, soon I hope, we'll meet,
and loneliness and sorrow will be history.

To be in the right place when you are there,
To dare and risk and hope to find you!
You must not hide nor fear nor hesitate
When chance and I come up behind you,

Or face you in a crowd, eyes meeting,
With people all around, and us apart.
I've got to be receptive to your being,
Allow you access to my mind and heart.

What's gone before, no matter how painful,
Must be laid aside when I meet you,
Because you and I will be a new beginning
of trust, hope, sharing, and being true.

I'll take the chance, my hoped-for darling,
And carpet your path with words and song,
so opportunity will actually enter;
you'll want to meet me, before long.

The door is open; I've prepared myself
For that thrill of recognition, near or far.
I'm ready, willing, waiting, and hoping;
Now, true love, how do I discover where you are?

Ursula T. Gibson, 6-16-88

## The Poet's Hope

If I can write your thoughts
in words you cannot say,
then I've done good
in freeing your mind to sing.

If I can sing your song
in tunes you cannot play,
then I've done good
helping your soul take wing.

If I can weep your sorrow
in tears you wish away,
then I've done good
by sincere enheartening.

If I can chant your hopes
in whispers you cannot pray,
then I've done good
to join your worshipping.

Ursula T. Gibson, 6-25-89; tweaked 8-4-89

## (Senryu)

"Hope springs eternal
in the human breast." Give boy
a fishing pole. See?

Ursula T. Gibson, 7-24-88

## Letting Go

Oh, you learn to let go.
First, it's a kitten—
one day, she's not there.
A dog got her, a coyote ate her,
she ran away and couldn't
find home again. You don't know why,
you can't find out. You cry,
you sorrow and fail to smile
for days and nights.
She's gone, and at last,
you see you have to let her go.

Then it's a friend—
you've shared bedrooms
and girl talk, you've whispered
to all hours of the night
together; you've stayed at
her house and she at yours,
and the moment you got home again,
you were on the telephone talking with her.
You've dreamed and feared together;
you've wondered and explored.
One person in the world
understands uncertainty.
But then, she moves, she's gone.
Letters fly, but there's no
eye contact, no giggles,
no hugs, no warmth, no her.
She's gone, and at last,
you see you have to let her go.

>>

Then it's a parent—
someone you've known all your life,
whose trust you care about,
whose honor you imitate,
whose standards you value—
suddenly not there,
suddenly unreachable
except by prayer.
And how those prayers stretch
to remember the voice, feel
the touch of nurturing hand,
wait for the recognition of self.
But that person is gone, and at last,
you see you have to let it go.

Then, it's your health that's gone—
no longer totally vigorous,
sometimes actually crippled,
unable to lift, to bend,
to hoe or rake or walk,
afraid of strain or physical pain,
afraid of effort that
makes the heart pound,
and the joy of running or
riding or making a breeze exist
no longer is part of living.
But that ability is gone, and at last,
you see you have to let it go.

Then it's job that's gone—
something you've worked at
all your adult life from
apprentice to expert,

from neophyte to professional,
you've slogged the road
and climbed the mountains;
you've given your all,
your input, your wisdom,
your training, your self,
and suddenly, it's gone.
You're unlikely to find
a substitute—too old, too lame,
and the decision to accept
retirement lies heavy on
your weary shoulders.
But that job is gone, and at last,
you see you have to let it go.


So, you learn to let go,
and you let go all through life
of persons and valuables,
of hopes and memories,
of dreams and possibilities,
until your world has narrowed
to its final scope,
a few more days, a few more hours,
and finally, a going that leaves
nothing left that must be let go.

Ursula T. Gibson © June 14, 2004

(This poem was selected as Best Poem of the San Gabriel
Poetry Quarterly, issue No. 24, July 12, 2004, $100.00)

# America

This country
where people laugh and cry
without looking around to see
who's keeping track of
their humor or their tears—

This country
where movement does not depend
on the good will of a border guard,
or location of the work unit and
the good will of the Party—

This country
where getting work depends on
skill, initiative, dependability,
not on whom you know in the Party or
whom you bribed enough—

This country
where checks and balances of power
keep individuals safer from might
of State, and the idea is the
best government is the least—

This country
where we review our history and
rewrite it in books and newspapers
as we discover truth instead of legend,
not the other way around—

This country
where all authority is questioned,
forced to justify its being, and
denied access to power if it
proves false or merely pompous—

This country
where freedom and responsibility
travel hand in hand, inseparable,
those who dodge one or the other
to attain an end being out of step—

This country
so ready to build, develop, alter,
tear down, reconstruct, invent, and
progress, yet worrying nationally
about dolphins, spotted owls—

This country
with contradictions at every crossing
and variety at every street corner,
seeking to belong to one nation,
to have a chance at light—

This country
where people boost each other upward
and step aside to honor dedication,
and each one has his work to do and
create his own dreams to dream—

This country,
the United States of America,
my chosen home, my beloved land,
my pleasure and grief, my haven and hope,
my past and my future—

God Bless You!

Ursula T. Gibson, 2002

## Tolerance

Ants in my parlor plants, trail away;
I don't want to kill you!
Moth in the reading lamp, flutter outside;
fly in the computer room, buzz elsewhere;
mosquito in the bedroom, hum another tune;
I don't want to kill you!
Cockroach in my kitchen? You—
Haven't got a prayer!!!

Ursula T. Gibson, 1988

# Biographical Sketch

Ursula T. Gibson, born May 4, 1930, in Munich Germany, came to the United States with her parents in 1934, and became a United States citizen on July 3, 1940. She says, "Boy, did we ever celebrate the Fourth of July that year!" During her college years, she was taught the art of oral interpretation by Dorothy Kaucher, Ph.D., and has practiced that art ever since. She has been the Poetry Editor for *Poetic Voices (www.poeticvoices.com)* since 1997, and reads between 150 and 300 poems a month to select those to be published in the on-line magazine that has a circulation of over 68,000 readers a month. She is a member and State Treasurer of California Federation of Chaparral Poets, Inc., and a member of California State Poetry Society. Her poetry has been published in journals and anthologies in the United States, Canada, Great Britain, Ireland, South Africa, and Australia, both in hard cover and on the Internet. She has published three chapbooks since 1990, *Eyes, Two Tujunga Poets*, and *Spirited*, including reading 48 poems from *Spirited* for a CD. She wrote a non-poetic book: *Be Prepared, Don't Mumble, Look UP! or How to Read Poetry Aloud*, published in 2003, to help those who wish to present their poetry most effectively in public. Ursula's mother died of heart failure in 1964; her famous father, Rudolf Schindler, M.D., died in 1980. Her brother, a civil engineer, eight years her senior, died in 1986. Ursula's son, Rudolf L. Shouldice, born December 1, 1953, died on April 11, 2000. Ursula and James Gibson, a professional astronomer, married on June 1, 1968, and have lived happily ever after in California, Connecticut, western Argentina, Bloemfontein, South Africa, and back to California. They are Tujunga, California, residents, together with their two ginger tabby cats, Edna and Quantum Jeffers, and three telescopes.

# INDEX

Printed in the United States
28754LVS00001B/264